VELOCITY

PERSONAL
STUDY
GUIDE

PURSUING THE
LIFE OF FAITH

Velocity
©2009
Billy Graham Evangelistic Association
1 Billy Graham Parkway
Charlotte, NC 28201-0001

CONTENTS

WHO IS JESUS CHRIST?

You may be picking up this book for several reasons. Are you a Christian who wants to grow in your faith? Or maybe you have just recently committed your life to Jesus Christ. Or you may simply be curious about what it means to have a relationship with Jesus Christ and want to know more. Jesus came to earth as God in human form. He came to enable us to have a relationship with Him—to bridge the gap between humanity and God.

This study will help you understand what it means to commit your life to Christ, have a real relationship with Him, and be sure of spending eternity in heaven with Him.

The first lesson in your study will deal with salvation, which simply means deliverance from sin and its consequences. The Holy Spirit works in your life when you have a relationship with Christ. In the lesson, you will find six verses from the Bible that teach us about salvation.

The first verse is found in Philippians 2:5–7: *"Christ Jesus: who, being in very nature God, did not consider equality with God something to be grasped, but made himself nothing, taking the very nature of a servant, being made in human likeness."* Jesus Christ, who has always existed as God, determined to come to earth so He could rescue us from our sins by dying on a cross. The birth of Christ was necessary so that He could be both God and human. Christmas is celebrated around the world as the birth of Christ. On Christmas we celebrate the direct intervention of God into human history. The other five verses deal with the process of the new birth of a believer in Christ.

Christ died for our sins according to the Scriptures, He was buried, and He was raised on the third day (1 Corinthians 15:3–4). Good Friday, signifying the death of Jesus, and Easter Sunday, the resurrection of Jesus, are likewise celebrated around the world.

Another step in the process of the new birth of a Christian is found in 2 Corinthians 5:21: *"God made him [Christ Jesus] who had no sin to be sin for us, so that in him [or through Christ Jesus] we might become the righteousness of God."* Right in God's sight—ready for heaven.

Another link is found in 1 Timothy 2:5–6: *"For there is one God and one mediator between God and men, the man Christ Jesus, who gave himself as a ransom for all men."* Picture a great chasm with you on one side and God on the other. The cross on which Jesus died bridges the gap. You cross that bridge through faith in Jesus.

Finally, *"Jesus did many other miraculous signs in the presence of his disciples, which are not recorded in this book. But these are written that you may believe that Jesus is the Christ, the Son of God, and that by believing you may have life in his name"* (John 20:30–31).

Go ahead—enjoy your lessons as you discover more about the Lord and Savior, Jesus Christ, and your daily walk with Him.

Velocity is a study featuring seven different topics with six Bible verses for each lesson. The Scriptures selected are basic to the Christian life and witness. This material can be used for personal devotions, one-on-one discipling of another, or for small group discussions.

Personal Devotions

Take one topic a week for seven weeks.
Take at least 15 minutes each day to ...

• Prayerfully read each verse.

• Circle key words or phrases. This will make you look more closely at the content of each verse.

• Answer the questions at the bottom of each page. You may want to use a separate sheet of paper or a small notebook for your written work.

• The verse study will give you a good look at some basic truth and specific insight to apply to everyday life.

• Memorize the verse in each lesson that is marked with an asterisk.

    Once you have finished the exercises you can start all over again. The second time, open your Bible and look at each verse in its context—reading the whole chapter from which the verse is taken.

One-On-One Discipleship

You can use this material for meeting with an individual for personalized follow-up. Have the individual complete the exercises on a weekly basis. When you meet, compare key words and phrases as well as answers to the questions. Discuss the application of these principles and have prayer together.

Small Group Study

The primary intention of these lessons is for small group interaction. A small group is a group of 6–12 people meeting weekly in an informal setting to study and discuss the Word of God. The leader asks questions to draw the group into a discussion of the Bible study, which each member of the group prepares in advance.

There is no perfect size for a small group nor a perfect number of weeks for the group to meet. But experience has taught a helpful guideline— avoid too many and too much! Six to twelve persons led for seven weeks can provide a wonderful learning experience—a journey of discovery!

The seven topics covered in this book are foundational to the Christian life: salvation, assurance, lordship, the Bible, prayer, the Holy Spirit, witness. In each lesson the Bible is the text and the Holy Spirit the teacher. All members of the group, including the leader, learn together. Indeed, every program of study must have a goal or objective. In each lesson in *Velocity*, we have three:

DISCOVERY
"What does God say?"

UNDERSTANDING
"What does the Scripture mean?"

APPLICATION
"How can this affect my life?"

Following is a suggested plan for Lesson One—Salvation—and a basic guide for Lessons Two to Seven.

Each participant will be discovering biblical truth by:

- Circling key words or phrases

- Answering questions

- Defining key words

- Paraphrasing a verse

- Making application to daily life

What is the purpose of *Velocity*?

The primary purpose is to follow up inquirers from an evangelistic event or a special outreach ministry. Following the evangelistic ministry, people who have made commitments, their friends, and other church members who are interested in Bible study should be invited to attend the small group.

Leadership and materials

Churches wishing to be in a small group ministry are responsible for training leaders. Copies of *Velocity*, a part of the Christian Growth Series, can be purchased at your local bookstore or through Grason in Charlotte, North Carolina, by phone: 1-800-487-0433, e-mail: grasoncs@bgea.org, or our Web site: **grason.org**.

Tips for leaders are in the back of the book, on pages 26–27. This section will be helpful in leading and organizing a study.

WEEK 1

0:00

Introduction/opening prayer
3–5 minutes

- The leader welcomes each member of the group and leads in an opening prayer.
- The leader then explains that the Bible study will cover seven lessons, with each lesson requiring about 75 minutes.

Get acquainted
10–15 minutes

- **Starting with the leader,** have each group member give his or her name and special interest.
  Example: Hobby; vacation; club activity; if a student, where? What program of study? etc.
- As each person shares, have each member write out the name and special interest on "My Group," page 11.
- Explain the importance of the six items under "As a member of the small group Bible study I will."

The lesson—discussion
25–30 minutes

- The leader reads aloud the introductory paragraph on "Salvation," page 12.
- The leader then reads aloud slowly and carefully the six verses printed on the page. As you read, have group members circle words and phrases that seem to "jump off the page," either as an insight into spiritual truth or as a question.
- Take two or three minutes for the group to silently reread the six verses.
- Ask question number 2. Discussion should follow after each question.

The lesson—verse study
15–20 minutes

Do the verse study on page 14. This will allow each group member to "dig deeper" into the subject of Salvation.

- Have each member define *believe* and *eternal life*.
- Ask if two or three members would like to share their definitions and have a brief discussion.
- Next, have each member paraphrase—that is, write in their own words—the verse John 3:16. Have two or three members read aloud their paraphrases and discuss.
- Next, have each member answer the question: How can you apply the truth of this verse to your life today? Note: This is usually more difficult in the beginning; therefore, the leader should set the pace by answering this question honestly and sensitively.

Home assignment
2 minutes

Give the following home assignment in preparation for Lesson 2, "Assurance."

- Have each group member read the introduction paragraph and verses prior to next week.
- Have each group member write out a question(s) they would like to ask the group next week.
- Encourage each member to memorize John 3:16—salvation. Memory verse cards are in the back of the book.

Closing comments/prayer
3 minutes

75:00

- Thank everyone for their participation, and lead in a closing prayer.
- Be careful not to put anyone on the spot by asking him or her to pray. Learning to pray out loud takes time. The leader should set a good example.

STUDY FORMAT

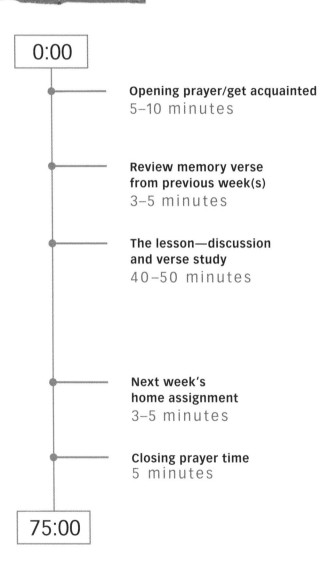

WEEKS 2-7

0:00

Opening prayer/get acquainted
5–10 minutes

Review memory verse
from previous week(s)
3–5 minutes

The lesson—discussion
and verse study
40–50 minutes

Next week's
home assignment
3–5 minutes

Closing prayer time
5 minutes

75:00

Names	Special Interest/Prayer Needs

_____

_____

_____

_____

_____

_____

_____

_____

As a member of this small group, I will:

1. Give priority to attending each week.

2. Faithfully complete the weekly home study assignments.

3. Participate in the group discussion as I am able.

4. Find creative ways to communicate my faith in Christ to others.

5. Pray by name for each member of my group during the weeks the group is meeting.

6. Refrain from discussing needs expressed in the group with anyone outside the group.

Signature: _____

Date: _____

SALVATION

Salvation means being rescued from sin and its consequence. Think about these truths until you can confidently say, "I know I am a Christian ... I have been born into God's family as His child ... I now have eternal life."

1. Circle key words and phrases in the following Scripture about Jesus.

Christ Jesus: Who, being in very nature God, did not consider equality with God something to be grasped, but made himself nothing, taking the very nature of a servant, being made in human likeness. And being found in appearance as a man, he humbled himself and became obedient to death—even death on a cross! **Philippians 2:5–8**

Circle key words and phrases in the following Scriptures about salvation.

But God demonstrates his own love for us in this: While we were still sinners, Christ died for us. **Romans 5:8**

For what I received I passed on to you as of first importance: that Christ died for our sins according to the Scriptures, that he was buried, that he was raised on the third day according to the Scriptures. **1 Corinthians 15:3–4**

For it is by grace you have been saved, through faith—and this not from yourselves, it is the gift of God—not by works, so that no one can boast. **Ephesians 2:8–9**

Circle key words and phrases in the following Scripture about becoming God's child.

Yet to all who received him, to those who believed in his name, he gave the right to become children of God—children born not of natural descent, nor of human decision or a husband's will, but born of God. **John 1:12–13**

Circle key words and phrases in the following Scripture about eternal life.

★ *For God so loved the world that he gave his one and only Son, that whoever believes in him shall not perish but have eternal life.* **John 3:16**

2. List what you learned about Jesus in

    Philippians 2:5–8 _____

    _____

List what you learned about salvation in

    Romans 5:8 _____

    _____

    1 Corinthians 15:3–4 _____

    _____

    Ephesians 2:8–9 _____

    _____

List what you learned about becoming God's child in

    John 1:12–13 _____

    _____

List what you learned about eternal life in

    John 3:16 _____

    _____

3. Do the verse study using the form on the next page.

Use the following verse to complete this verse study.

For God so loved the world that he gave his one and only Son, that whoever believes in him shall not perish but have eternal life. **John 3:16**

1. List two key words and define them.

Key Word _____

Definition _____

_____

Key Word _____

Definition _____

_____

2. What does the verse say?
(Paraphrase—rewrite the verse in your own words.)

_____

_____

_____

3. How can you apply the truth of this verse to your life today?

_____

_____

_____

Closing (Prayer time and assignment for next week)

4. Memorize John 3:16.

Memory verse card is in the back of this book.

Notes

_____

_____

_____

_____

_____

_____

One of Satan's tricks is to cause believers to doubt their salvation. Having assurance means being certain with a freedom from doubt. Meditate on the following Scriptures to enable you to have victory over your doubts.

1. Circle key words and phrases in the following Scripture about salvation.

In him we have redemption through his blood, the forgiveness of sins, in accordance with the riches of God's grace. **Ephesians 1:7**

Circle key words and phrases in the following Scriptures about why you can be sure.

Who through faith are shielded by God's power until the coming of the salvation that is ready to be revealed in the last time. **1 Peter 1:5**

I write these things to you who believe in the name of the Son of God so that you may know that you have eternal life. **1 John 5:13**

✱ *Being confident of this, that he who began a good work in you will carry it on to completion until the day of Christ Jesus.* **Philippians 1:6**

Circle key words and phrases in the following Scripture about Jesus.

For I am convinced that neither death nor life, neither angels nor demons, neither the present nor the future, nor any powers, neither height nor depth, nor anything else in all creation, will be able to separate us from the love of God that is in Christ Jesus our Lord. **Romans 8:38–39**

Circle key words and phrases in the following Scripture about who guarantees your salvation.

My sheep listen to my voice; I know them, and they follow me. I give them eternal life, and they shall never perish; no one can snatch them out of my hand. My Father, who has given them to me, is greater than all; no one can snatch them out of my Father's hand. **John 10:27–29**

2. List what you learned about salvation in

Ephesians 1:7 _____

_____

List what you learned about why you can be sure in

1 Peter 1:5 _____

_____

1 John 5:13 _____

_____

Philippians 1:6 _____

_____

List what you learned about Jesus in

Romans 8:38–39 _____

_____

List what you learned about who guarantees your salvation in

John 10:27–29 _____

_____

3. Do the verse study using the form on the next page.

Use the following verse to complete this verse study.

Being confident of this, that he who began a good work in you will carry it on to completion until the day of Christ Jesus. **Philippians 1:6**

1. List two key words and define them.

Key Word _____

Definition _____

_____

Key Word _____

Definition _____

_____

2. What does the verse say?
(Paraphrase—rewrite the verse in your own words.)

_____

_____

_____

3. How can you apply the truth of this verse to your life today?

_____

_____

_____

Closing (Prayer time and assignment for next week)

4. Memorize Philippians 1:6.

Memory verse card is in the back of this book.

Notes

When we place our faith in Jesus Christ, He becomes not only our Savior but also our Sovereign Lord and Master. We are under new ownership. We can only enjoy our new life in Christ as we daily seek His will and follow Him in obedience.

1. Circle key words and phrases in the following Scripture about new ownership.

Do you not know that your body is a temple of the Holy Spirit, who is in you, whom you have received from God? You are not your own; you were bought at a price. Therefore honor God with your body.
1 Corinthians 6:19–20

Circle key words and phrases in the following Scriptures about love and obedience.

Jesus replied: "'Love the Lord your God with all your heart and with all your soul and with all your mind.' This is the first and greatest commandment."
Matthew 22:37–38

Why do you call me, "Lord, Lord," and do not do what I say? **Luke 6:46**

Circle key words and phrases in the following Scriptures about priorities and benefits.

* *Delight yourself in the Lord and he will give you the desires of your heart. Commit your way to the Lord; trust in him and he will do this.*
Psalm 37:4–5

But seek first his kingdom and his righteousness, and all these things will be given to you as well. **Matthew 6:33**

Circle key words and phrases in the following Scripture about Jesus.

I am the vine; you are the branches. If a man remains in me and I in him, he will bear much fruit; apart from me you can do nothing. **John 15:5**

2. List what you learned about new ownership in

1 Corinthians 6:19–20 _____

_____

List what you learned about love and obedience in

Matthew 22:37–38 _____

_____

Luke 6:46 _____

_____

List what you learned about priorities and benefits in

Psalm 37:4–5 _____

_____

Matthew 6:33 _____

_____

List what you learned about Jesus in

John 15:5 _____

_____

3. Do the verse study using the form on the next page.

21

Use the following verse to complete this verse study.

Delight yourself in the Lord and he will give you the desires of your heart. Commit your way to the Lord; trust in him and he will do this. **Psalm 37:4–5**

1. List two key words and define them.

Key Word _____

Definition _____

_____

Key Word _____

Definition _____

_____

2. What does the verse say?
(Paraphrase—rewrite the verse in your own words.)

_____

_____

_____

3. How can you apply the truth of this verse to your life today?

_____

_____

_____

Closing (Prayer time and assignment for next week)

4. Memorize Psalm 37:4–5.

Memory verse card is in the back of this book.

Notes

To be the kind of Christians God wants us to be, we need to know and obey the Scriptures. Make it your habit to memorize and meditate on the Word of God daily.

1. Circle key words and phrases in the following Scripture about the Bible.

And how from infancy you have known the holy Scriptures, which are able to make you wise for salvation through faith in Christ Jesus. All Scripture is God-breathed and is useful for teaching, rebuking, correcting and training in righteousness. **2 Timothy 3:15–16**

Circle key words and phrases in the following Scriptures about the value of reading the Bible.

Your word is a lamp to my feet and a light for my path. **Psalm 119:105**

The unfolding of your words gives light; it gives understanding to the simple. **Psalm 119:130**

Great peace have they who love your law, and nothing can make them stumble. **Psalm 119:165**

Circle key words and phrases in the following Scripture about meditating on the Bible.

But his delight is in the law of the Lord, and on His law he meditates day and night. He is like a tree planted by streams of water, which yields its fruit in season and whose leaf does not wither. Whatever he does prospers. **Psalm 1:2–3**

Circle key words and phrases in the following Scripture about obedience.

★ *Do not merely listen to the word, and so deceive yourselves. Do what it says.* **James 1:22**

2. List what you learned about the Bible in

2 Timothy 3:15–16 _____

_____

List what you learned about the value of reading the Bible in

Psalm 119:105 _____

_____

Psalm 119:130 _____

_____

Psalm 119:165 _____

_____

List what you learned about the value of meditating on the Bible in

Psalm 1:2–3 _____

_____

List what you learned about obedience in

James 1:22 _____

_____

3. Do the verse study using the form on the next page.

Use the following verse to complete this verse study.

Do not merely listen to the Word, and so deceive yourselves. Do what it says. **James 1:22**

1. List two key words and define them.

Key Word _____

Definition _____

_____

Key Word _____

Definition _____

_____

2. What does the verse say?
(Paraphrase—rewrite the verse in your own words.)

_____

_____

_____

3. How can you apply the truth of this verse to your life today?

_____

_____

_____

Closing (Prayer time and assignment for next week)

4. Memorize James 1:22.

Memory verse card is in the back of this book.

Notes

_____

_____

_____

_____

_____

_____

PRAYER

Prayer is our lifeline to God. We need to form the habit of starting each day with prayer and then praying throughout the day.

1. Circle key words and phrases in the following Scriptures about prayer.

* *Until now you have not asked for anything in my name. Ask and you will receive, and your joy will be complete.* **John 16:24**

Ask and it will be given to you; seek and you will find; knock and the door will be opened to you. **Matthew 7:7**

Circle key words and phrases in the following Scriptures about God's power through prayer.

Now to him who is able to do immeasurably more than all we ask or imagine, according to his power that is at work within us. **Ephesians 3:20**

Call to me and I will answer you and tell you great and unsearchable things you do not know. **Jeremiah 33:3**

Circle key words and phrases in the following Scriptures about praying with confidence.

Dear friends, if our hearts do not condemn us, we have confidence before God and receive from him anything we ask, because we obey his commands and do what pleases him. **1 John 3:21–22**

This is the confidence we have in approaching God: that if we ask anything according to his will, he hears us. And if we know that he hears us—whatever we ask—we know that we have what we asked of him. **1 John 5:14–15**

2. List what you learned about prayer in

John 16:24 _____

_____

Matthew 7:7 _____

_____

List what you learned about God's power through prayer in

Ephesians 3:20 _____

_____

Jeremiah 33:3 _____

_____

List what you learned about praying with confidence in

1 John 3:21–22 _____

_____

1 John 5:14–15 _____

_____

3. Do the verse study using the form on the next page.

Use the following verse to complete this verse study.

Until now you have not asked for anything in my name. Ask and you will receive, and your joy will be complete. **John 16:24**

1. List two key words and define them.

Key Word _____

Definition _____

_____

Key Word _____

Definition _____

_____

2. What does the verse say?
(Paraphrase—rewrite the verse in your own words.)

_____

_____

_____

3. How can you apply the truth of this verse to your life today?

_____

_____

_____

Closing (Prayer time and assignment for next week)

4. Memorize John 16:24.

Memory verse card is in the back of this book.

Notes

_____

_____

_____

_____

_____

_____

God has not left us alone in the world. His Holy Spirit lives in us and daily ministers to our needs.

1. Circle key words and phrases in the following Scriptures about the Holy Spirit.

The wind blows wherever it pleases. You hear its sound, but you cannot tell where it comes from or where it is going. So it is with everyone born of the Spirit. John 3:8

Don't you know that you yourselves are God's temple and that God's Spirit lives in you? 1 Corinthians 3:16

* *But the Counselor, the Holy Spirit, whom the Father will send in my name, will teach you all things and will remind you of everything I have said to you. John 14:26*

Circle key words and phrases in the following Scriptures about being God's child.

The Spirit himself testifies with our spirit that we are God's children. Now if we are children, then we are heirs—heirs of God and co-heirs with Christ, if indeed we share in his sufferings in order that we may also share in his glory. Romans 8:16–17

Because those who are led by the Spirit of God are sons of God. Romans 8:14

Circle key words and phrases in the following Scripture about prayer.

In the same way, the Spirit helps us in our weakness. We do not know what we ought to pray for, but the Spirit himself intercedes for us with groans that words cannot express. Romans 8:26

WHAT DID YOU LEARN ABOUT:

2. List what you learned about the Holy Spirit in

John 3:8 _____

_____

1 Corinthians 3:16 _____

_____

John 14:26 _____

_____

List what you learned about being God's child in

Romans 8:16–17 _____

_____

Romans 8:14 _____

_____

List what you learned about prayer in

Romans 8:26 _____

_____

3. Do the verse study using the form on the next page.

Use the following verse to complete this verse study.

But the Counselor, the Holy Spirit, whom the Father will send in my name, will teach you all things and will remind you of everything I have said to you. **John 14:26**

1. List two key words and define them.

Key Word _____

Definition _____

_____

Key Word _____

Definition _____

_____

2. What does the verse say?
(Paraphrase—rewrite the verse in your own words.)

_____

_____

_____

3. How can you apply the truth of this verse to your life today?

_____

_____

_____

Closing (Prayer time and assignment for next week)

4. Memorize John 14:26.

Memory verse card is in the back of this book.

Notes

_____

_____

_____

_____

_____

_____

When we become children of God through faith in Jesus Christ, we become responsible to tell others about Christ. There is no greater privilege than sharing the love of God with your friends, family, and neighbors.

1. Circle key words and phrases in the following Scriptures about witnessing.

In the same way, let your light shine before men, that they may see your good deeds and praise your Father in heaven. **Matthew 5:16**

* *But in your hearts set apart Christ as Lord. Always be prepared to give an answer to everyone who asks you to give the reason for the hope that you have. But do this with gentleness and respect.* **1 Peter 3:15**

For we cannot help speaking about what we have seen and heard. ... Believe in the Lord Jesus, and you will be saved—you and your household. **Acts 4:20; 16:31**

Circle key words and phrases in the following Scripture about Jesus and witnessing.

"Come, follow me," Jesus said, "and I will make you fishers of men." **Matthew 4:19**

Circle key words and phrases in the following Scripture about the Holy Spirit and witnessing.

But you will receive power when the Holy Spirit comes on you; and you will be my witnesses in Jerusalem, and in all Judea and Samaria, and to the ends of the earth. **Acts 1:8**

Circle key words and phrases in the following Scripture about your responsibility.

We are therefore Christ's ambassadors, as though God were making his appeal through us. We implore you on Christ's behalf: Be reconciled to God. **2 Corinthians 5:20**

2. List what you learned about witnessing in

    Matthew 5:16 _____

    _____

    1 Peter 3:15 _____

    _____

    Acts 4:20; 16:31 _____

    _____

List what you learned about Jesus and witnessing in

    Matthew 4:19 _____

    _____

List what you learned about the Holy Spirit and witnessing in

    Acts 1:8 _____

    _____

List what you learned about your responsibility in

    2 Corinthians 5:20 _____

    _____

3. Do the verse study using the form on the next page.

Use the following verse to complete this verse study.

But in your hearts set apart Christ as Lord. Always be prepared to give an answer to everyone who asks you to give the reason for the hope that you have. But do this with gentleness and respect. ***1 Peter 3:15***

1. List two key words and define them.

Key Word _____

Definition _____

_____

Key Word _____

Definition _____

_____

2. What does the verse say?
(Paraphrase—rewrite the verse in your own words.)

_____

_____

_____

3. How can you apply the truth of this verse to your life today?

_____

_____

_____

Closing (Prayer time and assignment for next week)

4. Memorize 1 Peter 3:15.

Memory verse card is in the back of this book.

Notes

_____

_____

_____

_____

_____

_____

General Guidelines

1. The purpose of each lesson and verse study is to discover what God's Word says, to understand what it means, and to apply it to life.

2. A leader talks less than 20 percent of the time. Guide by skillfully using questions. Remember, this is not a lecture.

3. Maintain good eye contact by looking around the group and not focusing too much on one person.

4. The discussion of the lesson and verse study will take approximately 75 minutes. The leader divides the time between the questions and the verse study, emphasizing the importance of having a clear understanding of the important words. The leader keeps the group moving through the questions and the verse study.

5. A good leader will launch the discussion by using the suggested questions at the bottom of each section. Several additional questions may be used to guide the conversation.

> "What do others think about this?"
>
> "OK, what else?"
>
> If a pause (before someone responds) seems long, ask, "Does everyone understand?" If not, read the Scriptures and ask again.
>
> **Definition:** To clarify the meaning for the group—
> "What do we mean by _____?"
>
> **Illustration:** To relate concrete life situations—
> "How does this work out in life?"
> "Has anyone observed this? Tell us about it."
> "For example?"
>
> **Personalization:** Applying truth to your own life—
> "How have you experienced this?"

Concentration: Focus attention on the Word of God as the authority for our discussion and decisions.

"What other Scriptures help us here?"
"What Scriptures support this idea?"
"Turn to _____. How does this Scripture help us with our discussion?"

NOTE: You need not add any comment after a member speaks. Your silence implies neither approval of their reply nor disagreement with it.

Group Problems and What To Do About Them

1. Too Talkative:

- Ask: "What does someone else think?"
- Talk to them privately about the problem.
- Ask them to listen and ask questions to "help me out" in the next session.
- Assign them the project of listening to summarize.

2. Wrong Answers Given:

- Guide by letting the group comment or by having some more mature Christians in your group who can contribute a biblical foundation to your discussion.
- Ask: "What Scriptures help us here?" or "Let's look at _____ [reference] and see how this Scripture speaks to our discussion viewpoint."
- Counsel anyone with a special need privately after the meeting.

3. Noninvolved:

- Ask: "Anyone want to add something here?"
- "Just those who haven't spoken before on this question."
- Personal encouragement—take time alone with any reticent person.

4. Sidetracks:

- "Sometime that topic would be an interesting study, but right now the question is _____."
- Face the fact: "I think we're off track." Repeat the launch question for the section.

LEADER RESPONSIBILITIES

1. Form the Group.

- Recruit the members and issue invitations.

- Consult with pastoral leadership for suggestions. If your church has been involved in a special evangelistic event or ministry, a personal invitation should be given early to every inquirer who is referred to your local congregation. New members in your church should be included—your pastor may know of some with special needs.

- Invite personal friends and acquaintances. You may have friends in business or in the neighborhood who would add a different perspective to the group. Involve them.

- Find mature Christian friends who know and love the Word of God. They will greatly assist the group's understanding by contributing a biblical basis to the discussion.

- Allow for diversity of background among group members to aid the group's understanding.

2. Arrange practical details for the study.

Following are a few suggestions:

- Most successful programs are centered in a home. A home provides a warm and friendly atmosphere.

- Use a room not too small or too large for 6–12 people. Proper lighting, ventilation, and temperature are important.

- Seating should be in a circular pattern, with the circle complete if possible.

- Decide ahead of time who will take care of disturbances such as doorbells, telephones, and children.

- Serving refreshments is an option. If deemed appropriate, it should be after the study and clearly made optional for persons on a tight schedule.

- The small group Bible study format is designed for a 75-minute meeting. It is suggested that the study not run longer than this even though some individuals may want to spend additional time together.

- *Velocity* has been prepared to form the basis of discussion. The material is a guide—giving the format and discussion questions needed.

3. Manage time allotments.

Velocity has a suggested format including time allotments for each lesson. A good leader will attempt to give complete coverage to the material by setting the pace, moving the discussion along, and avoiding sidetrack issues.

4. Prepare.

- Do the study and complete the written answers.
- Make notes of additional questions that will be helpful to stimulate conversation.
- Pray regularly for each member of the group.

6. Let answers be given by all group members in a spontaneous pattern.

Don't call on specific people by name or go around the circle for answers.

7. A good question:

- Is never answered by "Yes" or "No."
- Has several replies.
- Is simple—easily understood.
- Is short—to the point.

8. Clarify answers or specific points.

To clarify the meaning of a specific point for the group, ask, "What do we mean by _____?"

9. Stick to the study form and topic.

If someone introduces some other subject, just say, "We can explore that some other time. Right now let's look at this study," and repeat a good discussion question.

10. **Make sure no one is dominating the discussion**.

If some people seem to dominate the discussion by talking too much, wait until they have finished and then ask, "What does someone else think about this?"

11. **Summarize each section in the study before moving on to the next section**.

"Does this cover the subject?"
"What is most meaningful about _____ (section title)?"
"What is the most valuable lesson from the section?"

Summary statements can be made:

By the Leader—Jot down notes of what is said. At the conclusion, put the main ideas together in a few sentences of summary.

By a Group Member—Leader assigns one member to summarize, or a question may be asked to evoke a summary:
"How would you summarize, in one sentence, what we have learned about _____[section's topic]?"

12. **Focus on personal application**.

Encourage the group members to make specific applications of the Scripture to their own lives.

13. **Help people who are not understanding key points**.

If someone is repeatedly misunderstanding key elements of the study, counsel that individual outside the group meeting.

- A sequence for memorizing:

  1. Topic   2. Verse   3. Reference

  The reference is like the handle on a suitcase, enabling you to lift up from the Bible a complete portion whenever needed.

- The real secret of Scripture memory is review, review, review.

- Quote the verse aloud. Ask God to make its meaning clear and applicable to you. Memorize one phrase at a time, using the reference, adding phrase by phrase until the entire verse is committed to memory.

Witness

"But in your hearts set apart Christ as Lord. Always be prepared to give an answer to everyone who asks you to give the reason for the hope that you have. But do this with gentleness and respect."
1 Peter 3:15, NIV

The Holy Spirit

"But the Counselor, the Holy Spirit, whom the Father will send in my name, will teach you all things and will remind you of everything I have said to you."
John 14:26, NIV

Prayer

"Until now you have not asked for anything in my name. Ask and you will receive, and your joy will be complete."
John 16:24, NIV

The Bible

"Do not merely listen to the word, and so deceive yourselves. Do what it says."
James 1:22, NIV

Lordship

"Delight yourself in the Lord and he will give you the desires of your heart. Commit your way to the Lord; trust in him and he will do this." ***Psalm 37:4–5, NIV***

Assurance

"Being confident of this, that he who began a good work in you will carry it on to completion until the day of Christ Jesus."
Philippians 1:6, NIV

Salvation

"For God so loved the world that he gave his one and only Son, that whoever believes in him shall not perish but have eternal life."
John 3:16, NIV

Witness

"But sanctify the Lord God in your hearts, and always be ready to give a defense to everyone who asks you a reason for the hope that is in you, with meekness and fear."
1 Peter 3:15, NKJV

7

Prayer

"Until now you have asked nothing in My name. Ask, and you will receive, that your joy may be full."
John 16:24, NKJV

5

The Holy Spirit

"But the Helper, the Holy Spirit, whom the Father will send in My name, He will teach you all things, and bring to your remembrance all things that I said to you."
John 14:26, NKJV

6

Lordship

"Delight yourself also in the Lord, and He shall give you the desires of your heart. Commit your way to the Lord, trust also in Him."
Psalm 37:4–5, NKJV

3

The Bible

"But be doers of the word, and not hearers only, deceiving yourselves."
James 1:22, NKJV

4

Salvation

"For God so loved the world that He gave His one and only begotten Son, that whoever believes in Him should not perish but have everlasting life."
John 3:16, NKJV

Assurance

"Being confident of this very thing, that He who has begun a good work in you will complete it until the day of Jesus Christ."
Philippians 1:6, NKJV